Cherubs
Angels of Love

Cherubs
Angels of Love

INTRODUCTION BY ALEXANDER NAGEL

THAMES AND HUDSON

First published in Great Britain in 1994
by Thames and Hudson Ltd, London

Conceived and produced by
Packaged Goods Incorporated
9 Murray Street
New York, New York 10007
A Quarto Company

British Library Cataloguing-in-Publication Data

A catalogue record for this book is available from the British Library

ISBN 0-500-01645-3

Art Director: Lesley Ehlers
Art and Text Research: Margaux King

Printed and bound in Hong Kong by Sing Cheong Printing Co. Ltd.

Acknowledgments

The author would like to thank Abraham Puchall, owner of the Herald Square Hotel, and Mary Clare Altenhofen, the reference librarian at Harvard University Fine Arts Library.

Special thanks from the designer and editor to the following tireless and invaluable contributors to this book: Dorothy Williams, Lindley Boegehold, Margaux King, Mariko Kato, Eric Jacobson, Mark Hill, Irene Rofheart-Pigott, Julia Gran, Janet Atkinson, Barry and Elyn Rosenthal, Frederic Winkowski, John Wilkes, Peter Michelena, Jeff Stem, Diana Faust, Greg Michaelson, Peter de Sève, Ford Rogers, Tina Klem, Sheila Callahan-Victore, Kate Donnelly, and Carolina Lascano.

In addition, a number of people offered special assistance in terms of art and resources. They are: Sarah Mitchell at Art Resource; Carole Lozoff at Everything Angels; Nadine Charlsen, researcher at Herald Square Hotel; Jaime Cardenas in the Commercial Office of the Peruvian Consulate; Danielle DiSpaltro at Packaged Goods Incorporated in San Francisco; Eileen Elias Freeman at AngelWatch; Margie McNaughton at Schumacher; Carol Curran and Tim Stevens at Recherché of Gramercy Park; Declan Spring and Griselda Ohannessian at New Directions Publishing Corporation; Inger of Sweden; and Seth Pariser at Christopher Hyland Incorporated.

Contents

Cherubs

An Introduction
Alexander Nagel

The winged, naked infant has haunted, delighted and uplifted the Western imagination from Hellenistic times to the present. In ancient times, they appeared as Cupids, intercessors of various kinds between humankind and the gods; in Christian art they assume the role of angels. The Italians refer to them all as *putti*, a word perhaps derived from the Latin *putus* for pure. The word "cherub" also serves a general function: We use it to describe not only the angels of Judeo-Christian theology but also Cupid and the other infant spirits known from pagan antiquity. This happy disregard for specific designation is very much in the spirit of the figure itself. The association with purity suggests the figure's elemental appeal, and helps to explain its persistent revival through the ages: its significance is so immediate to the human spirit that it exists, as it were, before any specific meaning is attached to it. It is a "deep" symbol that has been meaningfully interpreted at different times by different cultures and religions.

Curiously, however, it is in the nature of these figures to elude obedient participation in any one doctrinal system. Always the playful children, they toy with established symbols and maintain an irreverent aloofness from doctrine and theology. The cherub represents that eternal part of human nature that seeks relief from the burden of rigid structures of belief. The embodiment of a pure, "precultural" existence, the child laughs at our conventions and celebrates instead a spontaneous, natural wisdom.

To understand the significance of this figure we must therefore search beyond the confines of the traditional religious and mythological labels. Classical scholars have investigated the transformation of the figure of Eros from the winged adolescent figure of the classical period to the pudgy infant of later Antiquity. Biblical scholars and medievalists have, for their part, traced the "successive visions of the Cherubim," from the winged creatures described in the Old Testament and represented in Assyrian art, to the ethereal winged figures of the Christian Middle Ages, to the fleshy cherubs of the Renaissance. But few have investigated the common features, and thus the shared significance, of these infantile spirits themselves. The pudgy Cupid and the fleshy cherub are spiritual siblings, closer to each other than to their respective iconographic "parents." Ancient mythology and Christian theology might tell very different stories, but each visual tradition found a means to satisfy an ever-renewed fascination for these frolicking, fluttering babies.

The meaning of the cherub thus cannot be approached merely through the theology of the angel or the mythology of Eros. Indeed, those who study such matters tend to dismiss cherubs as nothing more than trivialized forms of more serious symbolic figures. Gunnar Berefelt, in his *Study on the Winged Angel*, for example, interprets the rise of the baby-like cherub in the Renaissance as evidence that "belief in angels was on the wane." The psychologist Erich Neumann, in his classic study of Eros and Psyche, likewise finds little to take seriously in the little Cupid: "...in the myth Psyche's lover and husband is the mighty, primordial god Eros, and not Amor or Cupid—the cunning little cherub known to us even from ancient works of art."

The scholars might take them less than seriously, but the human fascination with these pudgy-limbed, rosy-cheeked creatures never seems to fade. Indeed, they have never been more popular than they are today. Apart from their proliferation on prints, posters and notecards, they appear on earrings and keychains, they adorn frames, boxes, mugs and watches, they figure as candlesticks and even cookie cutters. This overflowing enthusiasm expresses a powerful spirituality, although of a singularly worldly sort. It is the open spirituality celebrated in Richard Wilbur's poem, "Love calls us to the things of this world:"

Outside the open window
The morning air is all awash with angels.
Some are in bed-sheets, some are in blouses,
Some are in smocks: but truly there they are.

The popularity of cherubs today is only the latest episode in a millennial history of cherub enthusiasm. Even the tendency towards kitschy multifariousness has typified the life of the cherub from the very beginning of its history. It has always been the focus of a popular enthusiasm, of a "cult" practiced on the margins of official religious orthodoxy, and, needless to say, almost always scorned by the arbiters of culture. Its mode of expression and its spirituality are not doctrinal, but directly linked to the charm of the objects themselves, to the special qualities of the many and various cherubs produced over the centuries.

To understand this fascination we must take the images themselves as our principal guide. How is the nature of the angel, or the god of love, affected by its incarnation in the form of a baby? What roles do these figures play and what tricks do they get up to in this infantile form? Whether they are Christian angels or the ministering spirits of Antiquity, their actual "performative" functions remain essentially the same. Like their ancient brothers, Christian cherubs act in ways that are typical of their infantile age, but at the same time reveal that they are instinct with a higher knowledge. It is precisely the contrast between their infancy and their motivated activity that produces their uncanny charm.

This effect elaborates upon the natural charm exerted by real-life toddlers. What most charms and fascinates us about toddlers is the staggering fact that they are people in miniature. We are quick to see in their

actions, whether intentional or not, the comic imitation of an adult activity—an imitation which almost always reflects ironically on ourselves. We love to attribute to them the possession of a knowledge they do not have. We are fascinated by the fact that such unformed beings possess, at some potential level, all the faculties that we do. This paradox is the cause of their unending charm and amusement for us. The combination of complete innocence with the capacity for knowledge separates them both from us and from the animal world. It irresistibly suggests the intervention of spiritual inspiration. The child's innocence is completed by something larger than all of us. The child suggests the presence of a mystery that tells us something about the limits of our "little life." It is for this reason that the figure of the baby, at least in the West, has assumed such a powerfully symbolic role, becoming a privileged intercessor between the worldly and the spiritual realms.

The figure of the cherub asserts that it is in the unencumbered joy of the infant that humankind is most prepared to enter into contact with the spiritual. In their innocent play cherubs embody a form of divine happiness that is inaccessible to most human beings. They mock the busy seriousness of our lives and they make light of the activity of the gods. They are, indeed, one of the most fruitful means developed by humankind to enter into dialogue with the spiritual realm.

The figure of the child plays a symbolic role in many cultures, but nowhere in so sustained and articulated a form as in the West. It in fact brings into striking relief those features that are characteristic of what we call the classical Western tradition. To perform its symbolic function, it is necessary that the cherub be anatomically recognizable as a child—that it have the palpable flesh of a baby—and that it behave in ways that are characteristic of that age. Only a tradition that makes naturalistic representation central to its symbolic language could generate and explore the full richness of such a figure. It is thus no surprise that the figure of the child has assumed symbolic importance in non-Western traditions marked by similar naturalistic concerns: Indian art, for example, which gives a vital role to qualities of physical corpulence, developed a cult around the image of the baby Krishna. Later, this implicit sympathy with Western tradition revealed itself in Mughal miniature painting, which showed great enthusiasm for incorporating European Renaissance cherubs within their traditional imagery.

The Putto in Antiquity

The earliest known *putti* go back to the fourth century BC. It is characteristic that they appear, from the beginning, in their canonical form and in great abundance. There are no stages in the emergence of the figure, no "archaic" phase where the figure is still in formation. They appear, as suddenly and as miraculously as newborn babies, and are immediately found in a variety of roles and on all sorts of objects. Their profusion is considered a characteristic feature of the style of this period, often described as "Hellenistic Rococo." They were from the beginning as common in the sphere of "decorative" art as in the more serious forms of religious and funerary iconography. Right away, they are found on earrings, pendants, rings, mirrors, belts and buckles, as well as on terracotta items more readily available to the lower classes. One earring from the second century BC, now in Brussels, shows a finely worked golden cherub holding a branch whose leaves are made up of little hearts—a charm to rival the most saccharine item from a modern sales catalogue. From its beginnings, the figure has trespassed playfully between the profane and the sacred, between the realm of kitschy decoration and the spiritual aspirations of "high" art.

In Antiquity the *putto* appears most often in settings presided over by Aphrodite and Dionysus, the gods of love and wine. In the realm of love, our Cupid is a younger version of the winged adolescent Eros known from earlier periods. Youth and tenderness have always been essential to the conception of the figure. In Plato's *Symposium*, the poet Agathon describes Eros as young, tender, delicate, moist, supple and languorous—qualities that are only further accentuated in the baby Eros. The great Greek scholar Jane Harrison observed that the figure of the winged Eros is a special form of the spirit figure known as the *Ker*. The Keres were the baleful wind-demons of evil and disease associated with the lusts of the flesh and often represented as swarms of tiny winged figures. Homer explicitly names this avenging angel the "Ker of death." The winged Eros represents the other side of the Ker's power; he is the "Ker of life." Where the Ker went downwards, deathwards, Eros, instinct with a new spirit, went upwards, lifewards. The two figures, split from the same principle, are striking analogues to the angels of Judeo-Christian tradition, some of whom, rebelling against God, were cast from heaven and became devils in the realm of hell. Is it a coincidence that, as St. Thomas Aquinas says, "The first angel who sinned is called, not a seraph, but a cherub" (or rather Kerub)?

In its infantile form, the figure is perhaps less threatening than the Ker-derived Eros, but he is no less powerful. In this form he only brings home with greater force of irony the eternal Virgilian truth that "Love conquers all." Everywhere that gods or mortals are led by their passions we are likely to see our little figure happily presiding over events. The late Antique writer Achilles Tatius of Alexandria begins his love story *Clitophon and Leucippe* with an extended description of a (fictional) painting of Zeus's rape of Europa. Nowhere has our figure been more congenially and sympathetically described:

> *Thus she was seated on the bull like a vessel under way, using the veil as a sail; about the bull dolphins gambolled. Cupids sported; they actually seem to move in the picture. Love himself led the bull–Love, in the guise of a tiny boy, his wings stretched out, wearing his quiver, his lighted torch in his hand: he was turning towards Zeus with a smile on his face as if he were laughing at him for his lighted torch in his hand: he was turning towards Zeus with a smile on his face as if he were laughing at him for becoming a bull for his sake. I was admiring the whole of the picture but–a lover myself paid particular attention to that part of it where Love was leading the bull. "Look," I said, "how that imp dominates over sky and land and sea!"*

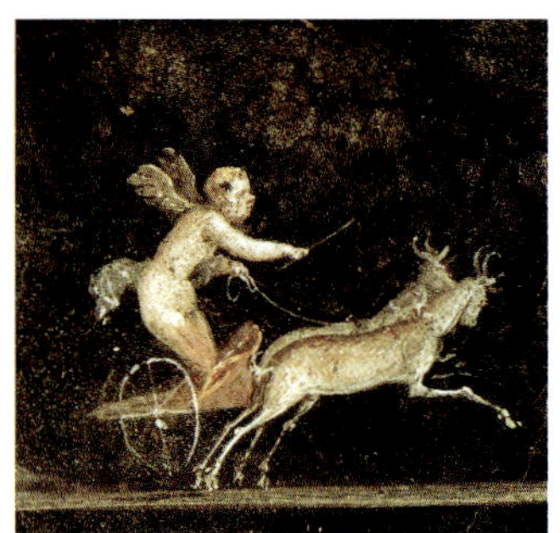

Cherub on a Chariot, detail, Pompeii, House of the Vetti

From the Hellenistic period onward the little figure of Amor predominates as facilitator and agent in countless scenes of fabulous love. He carries messages from the despondent Polyphemus to the nymph Galatea. He is the one to point out Helen to the wonderstruck Paris. He tugs on the drunken Bacchus's veil to direct his attention to the beautiful Ariadne, lying asleep on the shores of Naxos. With his torch he leads Selene to the beautiful sleeping Endymion, providing light even for the moon goddess. Other scenes show him actively unveiling the beloved in order to incite the lover. Often he literally sets the lover aflame with his torch. He moves the lover to bold and rash action, and then guides him through to its conclusion—conducting, for example, Pluto's chariot as it carries away Persephone.

The figure of Amor was almost irresistible to Roman decorative taste, and at once reveals it at its tawdriest and its most charming. A room in one of the wealthiest houses of Pompeii, the house of the Vetti, contains an entire suite of panels showing Amors fabricating the props and instruments of love: They gather flowers and then proceed to make and sell the garlands; they make perfume in a little laboratory complete with all the necessary instruments; as little goldsmiths they make jewelry; as weavers they make fine cloths; and finally as vintners they make and sell wine, the liquor of love.

This last activity suggests how a connection could be forged between the realm of Aphrodite and the realm of Dionysus, the other principal arena in which the *putto* predominated. He is shown accompanying the wine-god himself, or in association with his followers. Together with his many little friends, he carries the drunken Pan and rides upon the centaurs and satyrs. He prepares the dionysian banquet. He brandishes

The River Nile, Rome, Vatican

Dionysus' thyrsus and plays music while the maenads dance. In his unassuming form, he takes the attendants unawares and fills them with the spirit of the god: He is the awakener of dionysian joy, the personification of frenzy and desire. In his double function as Eros he attends to Dionysus's lover Ariadne. He is often shown paying reverence to statues of Dionysus, bringing him offerings, crowning his head or festooning him with garlands. Indeed, the baby Dionysus, who was classically represented in the fifth century BC by Praxiteles in the arms of Hermes, was one of the earliest incarnations of the *putto*. It is often difficult to know in dionysian scenes whether a baby figure is a *putto* or the god himself.

Cherub With Garlands, detail, Pompeii, House of the Vetti

Conceived in the company of Aphrodite and Dionysus, the *putto* is a fulsome, inevitable attendant in the realm of love and ecstasy. Through this realm he was in turn profoundly connected to the mysteries of fertility and regeneration. The connection is made explicit in the famous sculpture of the River Nile in the Vatican museum. The Nile, the bringer of fertility to the Egyptian plains, is shown passively reclining while hordes of *putti* clamber all over his massive figure. These associations also produced the very common figure of the *putto* holding a cornucopia, symbol of abundance. Love connects humankind to the forces of life, and thus our little Amor is in continual contact with the elements of nature. He is especially fond of animals, as children typically are; he is shown playing with birds, riding horses and elephants, romping with the panthers and lions of the Dionysian *thiasos*, and jet-skiing on dolphins or other marine animals.

Above all, however, the figure flourished in the world of vegetal growth. Countless sarcophagi, or marble coffins, show reliefs of *putti* holding heavily laden swags, trophies of overflowing nature gathered into decorative form. They also appear with great frequency on sarcophagi representing the seasons, which were popular especially from the time of the Emperor Hadrian. As representations of the cycles of time and regeneration, the images of the seasons were prevalent especially in the context of funerary art. Perhaps as a result of their special associations with dionysian cults, the most popular of these images were those that showed the *putti* in the role of vintners, gathering the harvest, crushing the grapes, and making the wine. In this setting, dominated by concerns about the afterlife, the activity of the vintage becomes a complex allegory on the attainment of the afterlife—the soul is released from the mortal body just as the wine is born from the breaking open of the grape.

The Putto as Intercessor

Grape Harvest, Rome, Santa Costanza

This imagery was, needless to say, well-suited to the wine symbolism of the Christian faith, and it is in the context of vintage imagery that *putti* make their appearance in some of the most important antique Christian monuments. Several early Christian sarcophagi show the *putti* of the wine harvest in association with other Christian symbols, such as the "Good Shepherd" holding the lamb. In the famous vault mosaics of Santa Costanza, an early Christian church of the mid-fourth century in Rome, they are shown again amidst grape vines. A famous porphyry sarcophagus which originally stood in the very same sanctuary, and which held the body of Constantina (the daughter of the first Roman emperor Constantine), proudly displays them in *rinceaux* (wreaths) of grape vines, as they harvest the grapes and make the wine.

On both Christian and pagan sarcophagi, as well as in other kinds of monuments, the *putto* often serves an intercessory function. He is a true *amicus humani generis,* a friend of the human race, facilitating communication with the spiritual realm. Often he is shown standing on the corners of the sarcophagus with a melancholy expression and his torch turned upside down—a mourner for the dead. On countless sarcophagi pairs of flying *putti* hold a roundel with an image of the deceased, the *imago clipetea,* symbolizing his or her ascent to the heavens. They are shown watching over the deceased, crowning him or bringing offerings of flowers. In more active scenes *putti* drive the deceased heavenward in a dove-drawn chariot. In a typical fusion of the playful and the sacred, his ride upon the backs of marine animals can take on the further dimension of a sea-voyage to the life beyond.

As mediator between humankind and the gods, Amor is prevalent in cultic and sacrificial settings. Since Hellenistic times, he was represented as an assistant, helping in the act of sacrifice: He carries plates of offerings, he makes libations, he offers at the altar. In the Villa of the Mysteries at Pompeii, an Amor pushes a small pig toward the altar to be sacrificed to Priapus. Similar sacrifices by Amoretti occur in the House of the Labyrinth. Some scholars have seen in these images reflections of the actual practice of using children as servants at the sacrifice, although it is known that the adolescent Eros of classical Greek times also fulfilled this function. However that may be, it is clear that Amor is continually given a special license to toy with the instruments of divine power. He is often shown playing with the attributes of the other gods—an indication of his power and influence over them. He serves them, but he also mocks them and through this comic activity makes them more accessible to humankind. He is shown playing with Neptune's trident or Jupiter's thunderbolt, brandishing Mercury's caduceus or Bacchus's thyrsus, sporting Hercules' lion skin or playing Apollo's lyre.

This function as mediator gives his simple attendance upon a scene of love, especially in a funerary setting, a further symbolic dimension. Take for example sarcophagi that depict the story of Endymion. Endymion, condemned to eternal slumber after being granted the gift of perpetual youth, was visited nightly by the moon-goddess Selene. Eternal youth is thus held in the embrace of Sleep—always a powerful metaphor for death—and is brought into ever-renewed congress with the divine. The theme had powerful associations in a context fraught with the aspiration to attain immortality in the afterlife. As the crucial agent and presiding spirit of the scene, the figure of Amor not only facilitates a scene of love, but effectuates its translation onto this further symbolic plane.

In many ways, therefore, our little Amor functioned as a symbolic mediator, drawing forth associations between different arenas of meaning. He establishes connections between the Aphrodisiac and the Dionysian realms, and then between them and the mysterious processes of fertility and regeneration. In general he is there to facilitate the union between human and divine, between the natural world and the spiritual forces that govern it. He is a malleable thematic mortar, bringing discrete elements into new and powerful union. Is this not, in the end, the essence of love's power?

The *putto* went into decline during the period we call the Middle Ages. He had appeared, as we have seen, on some early Christian monuments, where his symbolic associations were adapted to the tenets of the Christian faith. Thereafter he appears in sculpted decorative elements on monuments clearly influenced by the antique, such as the facade of the cathedral of Modena or Siena, or the architectural decoration of the cloister at Monreale. A more "motivated" use of the figure, reviving it within new thematic contexts, occurs after 1300 in Italy. It is only then, for example, that the figure is reconceived as an angel. Lone and prophetic episodes of such appropriation are, however, known from the earlier period. We know of a thirteenth-century abbot of the monastery of St. Etienne at Caen in France, who reinterpreted an antique gem of a *putto* in this manner. Around it he engraved the verse from St. Matthew in which God the Father announces at the Annunciation, *"Ecce mitto angelum meum* (Behold I

Francesco Traini, *The Triumph of Death,* Pisa, Camposanto

send my angel)." Knowing full well that it was a pagan gem, the abbot nonetheless saw in the figure the potential for a new role suited to Christian belief.

The Renaissance Cherub

Only eventually did painters fulfill this project of appropriation. When, after 1300, the figure begins to appear with some frequency in Christian scenes it is still very much quoted as an antique *putto.* In Giotto's fresco, *The Birth of the Virgin,* painted ca. 1310 in the Arena Chapel in Padua, the building shows a pediment relief of two flying *putti* holding a roundel bust of Christ, just as they hold the *imago clipetea* on ancient sarcophagi. In Francesco Traini's somewhat later fresco of the *Triumph of Death,* in the Camposanto at Pisa, the torch-wielding Amor of Antiquity reappears in something like his original function, although now under the more somber cast of late-medieval death imagery: He descends upon two unsuspecting lovers, and with inverted torch announces their impending end.

It was not until the fifteenth century that the conception of the prescient French abbot was realized, and the *putto* found a new role as a Christian angel. Traditionally angels had been represented as long, draped, ethereal figures in flowing robes, a type derived from the ancient figure of Victory. The introduction of the baby cherub among the ranks of the angels in a sense fulfills the etymology of the word itself: Most Jewish and Christian authors took the first part of the word (che) to mean "like" and the second part (rub) to mean "infant" or "young boy"—thus "like children."

If any one artist is responsible for having propagated the new type it was the Florentine sculptor Donatello. He gave the antique form a new motivation within the Christian context. His famous *Cantorium* for Florence Cathedral, which served as a balcony from which the church musicians and singers played and sang, shows a multitude of dancing cherubs, celebrating the joys of divine music. He drew upon the energy of the ancient Amor and thus discovered a new dimension within Christian spirituality. After Donatello, it became virtually *de rigueur* for up-to-date artists to depict angels in this form. Those artists influenced by Donatello in northern Italy, such as Giovanni Bellini and Andrea Mantegna, as well as those who followed him in Florence, made cherubs a standard accoutrement of the Christian image-repertoire. Cherubs float above the Madonna and Child, attend to the Christ child, or play musical instruments on the steps of her throne. They are even shown in scenes of the Passion, lamenting over Christ's death.

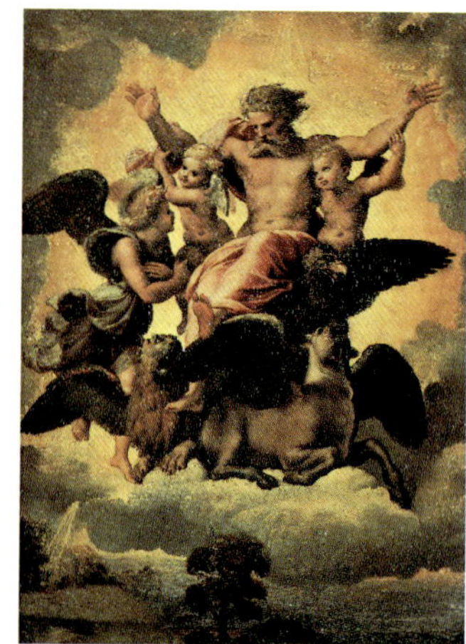

Raphael, *The Vision of Ezekiel,* Florence, Pitti Palace

It is curious that the age that saw the rise of the cherub was also

Raphael, *detail of Sistine Madonna,* Dresden, Gemäldegalerie

marked by the growth of a new devotion to the Christ child. In the place of the hieratic Virgins of the Middle Ages, Renaissance painters depicted increasingly tender scenes of affectionate love between mother and son. Images of the Christ child alone, independent of the Virgin, also appeared and became the focus of a new, extremely sentimental devotion. The enthusiasm that fed the proliferation of the child-like cherub thus also generated the cult of the Bambino Gesù.

Raphael, *Madonna of Foligno,* Rome, Vatican, Pinacoteca

Through the fifteenth century, the image of the cherub still retained the quality of a figure revived from ancient art. It was used by painters and sculptors working in a consciously *all'antica* style. It was not until shortly after 1500, in the art of Raphael, that the figure achieved full "naturalization" within the Christian context. In Raphael we no longer think of the figure's derivation from the ancient Amor; it has attained its own substantiality as a natural incarnation of the Christian angel. Raphael's cherubs form the very basis of our ability to visualize these beings, and all later cherubs are in some way their descendants. This perhaps explains why Raphael's angels have never become mere relics of past art, and instead continually play an active role in the art of later eras. The two cherubs leaning on the parapet at the bottom of the *Sistine Madonna,* for example, have effectively become superstars of our contemporary visual culture.

Raphael, *The Triumph of Galatea,* Rome, Villa Farnesina

Raphael clearly identified his cherubs with the cherubim described in the Old Testament. In his small painting of the *Vision of Ezekiel,* for example, he ignores the prophet's description of the cherubim as fantastic composite creatures, and depicts them as two baby cherubs like those we know from his other works. These, for Raphael, are the cherubs described in the passage from Psalms 18: 9-10: "He bent the heavens and came down,/ a dark cloud under his feet;/ he mounted a cherub and flew,/ and soared on the wings of the wind." It was also Raphael who affirmed the essential identity between the Christian cherub and the Cupid of pagan mythology. He makes no effort to distinguish, in form or manner, the angel who holds the tablet in his *Madonna of Foligno* from the cupids who cavort around *Galatea.* The same identification occurs in Titian, whose cherubs were strongly influenced by Raphael's: The angels that carry aloft the Virgin of the *Assumption* are for all the world the same beings who play and romp as Cupids in the exactly contemporary *Worship of Venus.* Having brought the figures to this new level of realization, Raphael and Titian discovered the essential identity of their spiritual function.

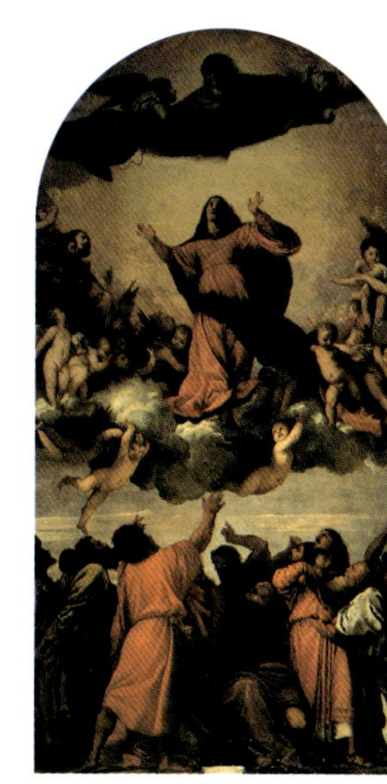

Titian, *Assumption of the Virgin,* Venice, Santa Maria Gloriosa dei Frari

Michelangelo also affirmed the profound spiritual affinity of all these infant figures, to the extent

Michelangelo, *The Prophet Isaiah,* Rome, Vatican, Sistine Chapel

Michelangelo, *Bacchanal of the Children,* Windsor, Windsor Castle

that he refused even to respect the nominal differences between them. For him, the Judeo-Christian angel was nothing more than a form of the antique genius figure, the figure who guides, protects and brings divine inspiration. These are the beings who whisper into the ears of the prophets on the Sistine ceiling. They are less playful than Raphael's cherubs, and are more exclusively dedicated to their role as conduits of divine wisdom. It was Michelangelo who explored the graver, "deeper" side of the *putto's* significance. The work that launched his career in Rome was a sculpture of the sleeping Cupid, which he artificially weathered and passed off as an antique. It was this more somber dimension of the figure that he explored in the later drawing *Bacchanal of the Children,* in which the lugubrious quality of the figure's Dionysian association predominates. It is a conception in stark contrast to the sunny and playful host of Cupids depicted in Titian's *Worship of Venus.*

The tradition of Raphael and Titian nonetheless prevailed, and inspired the proliferation of cherubs in later Renaissance and Baroque art. The extent of this proliferation can be gathered from the illustrations that appear in this book. This tradition was to find its greatest exponent in Rubens, whose art is virtually symbolized by the rosy-cheeked, fleshy-limbed cherub. The Mannerist, Baroque and Rococo periods spread Italianate style throughout Europe, and carried the cherubs with them. In the North, and especially in Germany, the figure flourished above all in sculptural form. How many German Baroque and Rococo churches are filled with hosts of frothy sculpted cherubs rising through the architecture?

Victoriana and More Recent Revivals

Cherubs again went into decline with the waning of the Rococo style, but in the Victorian era they underwent another revival, this time in a clearly nostalgic and sentimental vein. What marks this era is less the cherubs that were produced than those that were *re*produced: Greeting cards and valentines made up of printed reproductions of cherubs and cupids were the order of the day. They assumed the proportions of elaborate paper confections, involving cut-outs and embossed figures known in England as "scraps." But the decorative dissemination of cherubs was not confined to paper. In one of the best-selling novels of the period, Wilkie Collins' *The Moonstone*, the two lovers, Franklin and Rachel, together paint a boudoir door with "patterns and devices—griffins, birds, flowers, cupids and such like." The door, needless to say, becomes a crucial element in the mystery of the Moonstone and in the story of their love. Typically, the motifs are "copied from designs made by a famous Italian painter, whose name escapes me: the one, I mean, who stocked the world with Virgin Maries, and had a sweetheart at the baker's." (He means, of course, Raphael.)

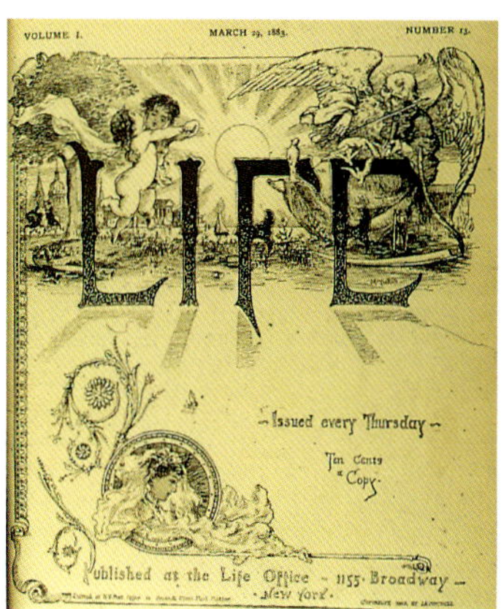

Life magazine cover, March 29, 1883

The era's love for the cherub was consummated in a publication produced in the United States, *Life* magazine. The magazine was founded by John Ames Mitchell in 1883 on the principle that wisdom can be found in fun. For Mitchell, the figure that most clearly embodied that principle was the cherub. Before beginning the magazine he had published a book of his own illustrations entitled *The Summer School of Philosophy at Mt. Desert*, in which Cupids teach the "students"—young and amorous couples—in the wisdom of love. When he came to publish the magazine, Mitchell designed a cover which shows two cherubs dancing to the tune played by Time: They are the figure of life itself. Themes of love, mingled with occult philosophy, run through all of Mitchell's many novels, but for him all these ideas found their ultimate expression in the simplicity and purity of the cherub. When in 1893 he built a new headquarters for *Life* at 19 West 31 Street in New York City, he commissioned from the sculptor Philip Martiny a figure of a cherub, called the *Winged Life*, to be placed on the pediment over the principal door. (It is still there, and has been newly gilded.) In a slightly later novel, *That First Affair*, the figure itself, curiously cast in the role usually reserved for the serpent in the garden of Eden, is made to speak: "I am the essence of all men—of the millions yet unborn. I am the sap and soul of human life, the realization of lovers' dreams. I am the absorbing and resistless passion; the one undying thing; the everlasting joy and torture. That's what I am!"

The Modernist movement, in many ways a formal backlash against the softer forms of nineteenth-century taste, effectively banished cherubs from artistic expression during most of the twentieth century. Recently, however, enthusiasm for cherubs has surged yet again. They are cropping up, as is their wont, in great abundance and in the most diverse forms of decoration. It is already possible to imagine future historians classifying this resurgence as part of a "late twentieth-century Rococo style." As in the earlier periods, the present-day enthusiasm for cherubs combines utter kitsch with sincere spirituality. Cherubs provide moments of sentiment and spirituality in a world increasingly devoid of them. It is perhaps precisely their easy appeal and their marketability that make them a viable carrier of spiritual meaning in today's world. But this is not simply a case of spirituality "cheapened" by commercial proliferation. The cherub's special power and significance are due precisely to its exuberant participation in all aspects of human life. The cherub will always mingle sacred things with profane, and for this reason will always be reborn.

In the Heavens

Heaven is large, and affords space for all modes of love and fortitude.

Ralph Waldo Emerson

It is not by age
but by disposition that
wisdom is reached

Plautus

Non aetate verum
ingenio adipiscitur
sapientia

*Non aetate verum
ingenio adipiscitur
sapientia*

Whether the angels play only Bach in praising God, I am not sure; I am sure, however that en famille *they play Mozart.*

Karl Barth

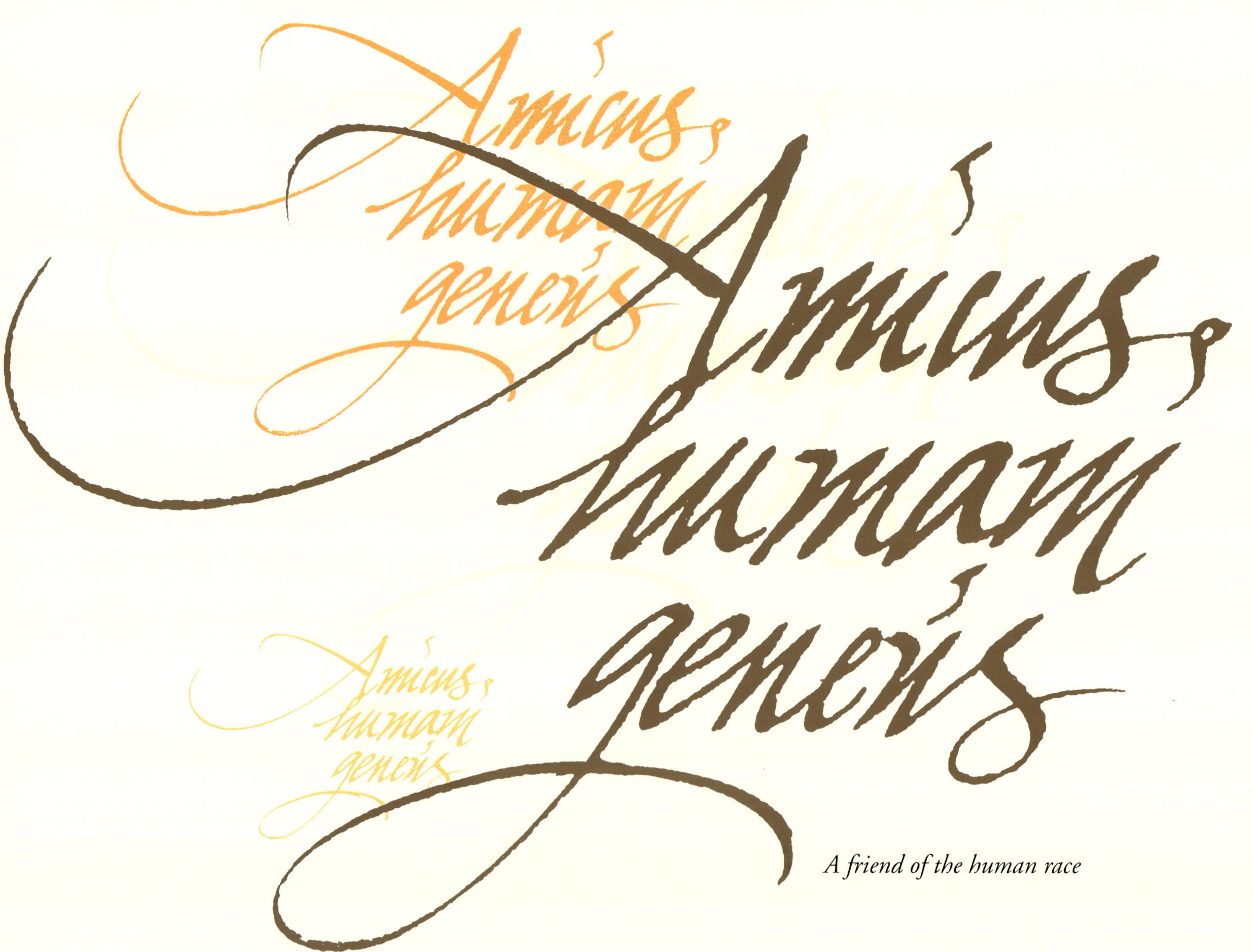

A friend of the human race

PAX · HOMINIBVS
LAVDA

Cupid is naked and does not like artifices contrived by beauty.

Propertius

Visits and Messengers

Their line is gone out through all the earth, and their words to the end of the world.

Book of Psalms 19:4

Sobieskys Schild
Südl. Krone
Antinous
Steinbock
Luftpumpe

*Their line is gone out
through all the earth,
and their words to the
end of the world.*
Book of Psalms 19:4

Südl. Krone
Sobieskys Schild
Steinbock
Mikro
Luftpumpe

Gr. Wolke
Kl. Wolke
Eridanus
Georgsharfe
Herbstnachtgleiche
September
October
Spica
Kornähre
März

We are near awakening when we dream that we dream

Baron Friedrich von Hardenberg

عمل گوردهن

Love to faults is always blind,
Always is to joy inclined,
Lawless, winged, and unconfined,
And breaks all chains from every mind.

William Blake

Love, all alike, no season knows, nor clime,
Nor hours, days, months, which are the rags of time.

John Donne

LIFE

Every man hath a good
and
a bad angel attending
on him in
particular all his life long

Robert Burton

And yet, as Angels in some brighter dreams
   Call to the soul, when man doth sleep:
So some strange thoughts transcend our wonted theams,
   And into glory peeps.

If a star were confin'd into a Tomb
   Her captive flames must needs burn there;
But when the hand that lockt her up, gives room,
   She'll shine through all the sphaere.

O Father of eternal life, and all
   Created glories under thee!
Resume thy spirit from this world of thrall
   Into true liberty.

Henry Vaughan

Music and Dance

And tell the stars, and tell you rising sun
Earth, with her thousand voices, praise God
Samuel Taylor Coleridge

I want to be an angel.
And with the angels stand,
A crown upon my forehead,
A harp within my hand
Urania Bailey

Music is well said
to be the speech of angels.

Thomas Carlyle

In Heaven a spirit doth dwell
"Whose heart-strings are a lute;"
None sing so wildy well
As the angel Israfel,
And the giddy stars (so legends tell)
Ceasing their hymns, attend the spell
Of his voice, all mute.

Edgar Allan Poe

As sweet and musical

As bright Apollo's lute, strung with his hair;

And when Love speaks, the voice of all the gods

makes heaven drowsy with the harmony

Shakespeare

Every Morne from hence,
A brisk Cherub something sips,
Whose sacred influence
Adds sweetnes to his sweetest lips
Then to his Musick, and his song
Tastes of his breakefast all day long

Richard Crashaw

Lovers and Fertility

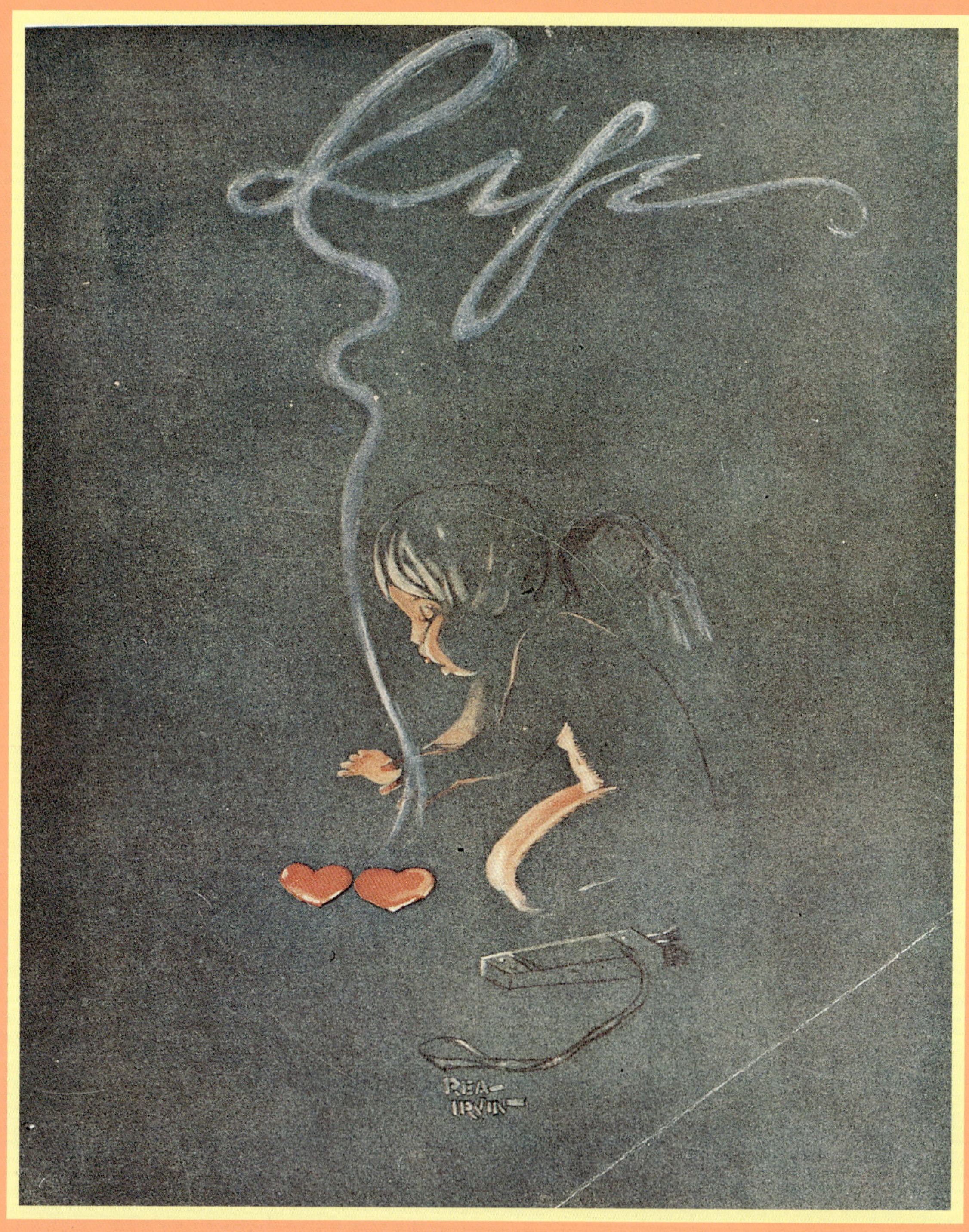
Life
REA
IRVIN

TO MY
Valentine
Though Cupid's aim
is true
And piercing is his dart,
I shall not mind, if you
Will give to me,
your heart.

*The human race
is organized like the bees;
the feminine is a queen,
infinitely fertile.*

George Santayana

In the time when herbs and flowers,
Springing out of melting powers,
Teach the earth that heat and rain
Do make Cupid live again.

Fulke Greville

Be fruitful and multiply,

and replenish the earth

Book of Genesis 1:28

Love looks not with the eyes,
but with the mind,
And therefore is winged Cupid
painted blind.

Shakespeare

Sweet Cupid's shafts, like destiny,
Doth causeless good or ill decree.
Desert is born out of his bow,
Reward upon his wing doth go.
What fools are they that have not known
That Love likes no laws but his own!

Fulke Greville

All we know

Of what they do above,

Is that they happy are,

and that they love.

Edmund Waller

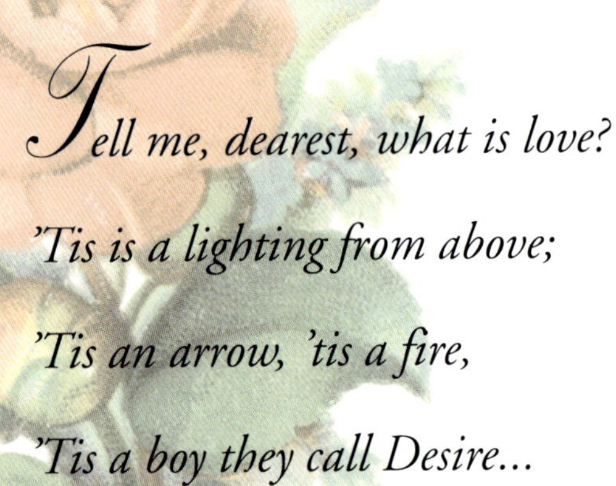

Tell me, dearest, what is love?

'Tis is a lighting from above;

'Tis an arrow, 'tis a fire,

'Tis a boy they call Desire...

John Fletcher

le 10
Vandemiere
an 6.

To my Valentine
Cupid's roving, plucking roses,
Lo! in one a bee reposes.

Mischief and Play

Plump little Cupid sits in the cold,
Troubling the air with a woeful din,
But if to comfort him you make bold,
You'll be the one to be taken in.
Life magazine

93

What should we be without

The dolphin's arc, the dove's return…

These things in which we have seen

ourselves and spoken?

Richard Wilbur

God is love....

But what a mischievous

devil Love is!

Samuel Butler

3 more novels of
Ronald firbank
3 more novels of Ronald firbank
Caprice
vainglory
inclinations

In the sun that is
young once only,
Time let me play and be

Dylan Thomas

Cupid Fallen

The wind blew little Cupid down last night
who, in the dim nook of the park, with guile
bending his bow, would watch us with a smile,
and give us a long day of dream-delight,

Last night's wind blew him down. Ah! sad to see
the broken marble at the breath of dawn,
scattered, the artist's faint-seen name upon
the base, among the shadows of a tree.

Oh, it is sad, this empty base of stone,
and melancholy fancies enter in
and wander through my dream where deep chagrin
calls up a future fated and alone.

Oh, sad!—And you yourself, yes? feel the pain
of this drear picture, though your frivolous eye
toys with the gold-and-crimson butterfly
fluttering above the fragments in the lane.

Paul Verlaine

Neither a lofty degree of intelligence
nor imagination nor both together
go to the making of genius.
Love, love, love, that is the soul of genius.

Attributed to Wolfgang Amadeus Mozart

The Cherub Explained

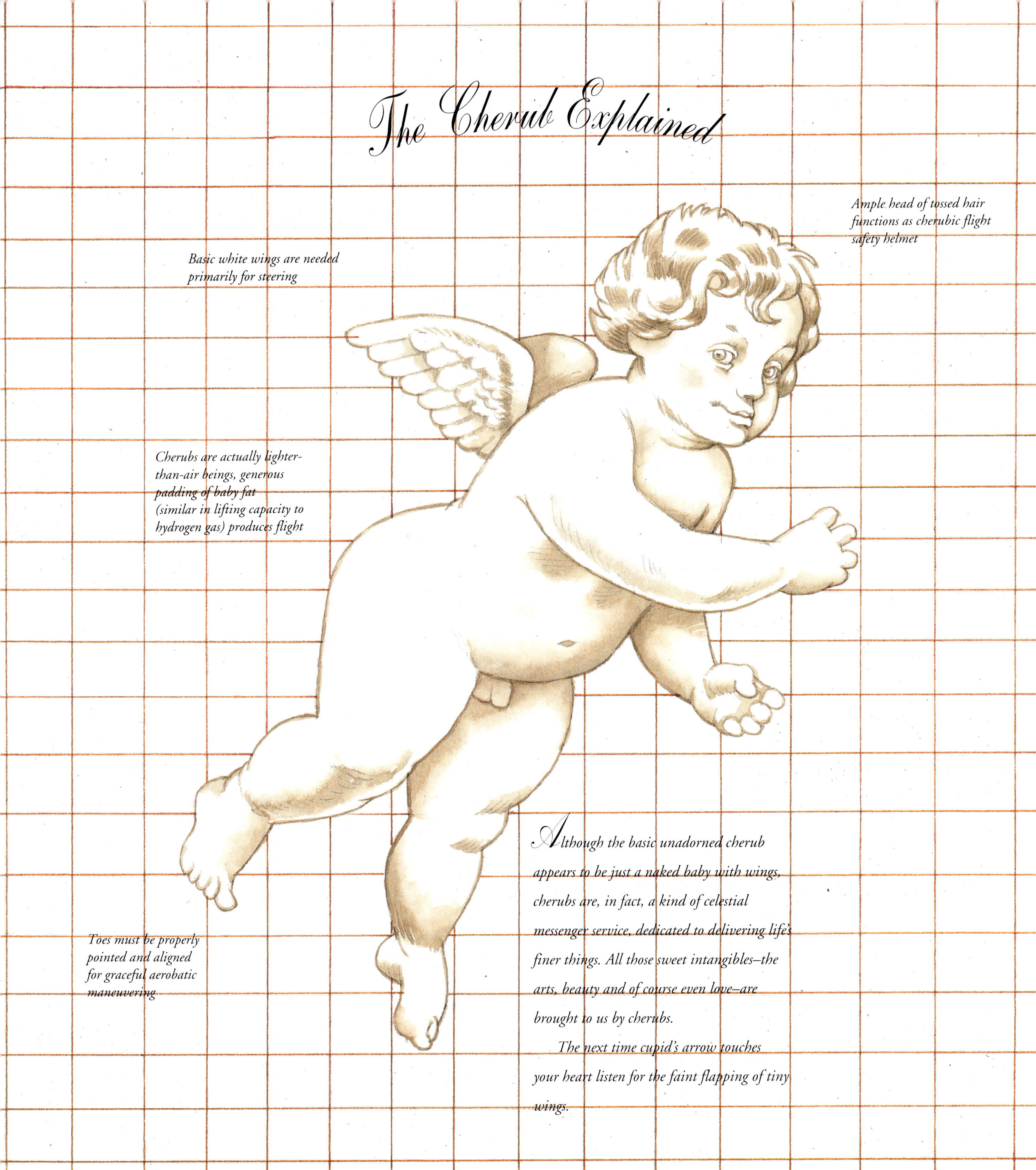

Ample head of tossed hair functions as cherubic flight safety helmet
Basic white wings are needed primarily for steering
Cherubs are actually lighter-than-air beings, generous padding of baby fat (similar in lifting capacity to hydrogen gas) produces flight
Toes must be properly pointed and aligned for graceful aerobatic maneuvering

Although the basic unadorned cherub appears to be just a naked baby with wings, cherubs are, in fact, a kind of celestial messenger service, dedicated to delivering life's finer things. All those sweet intangibles–the arts, beauty and of course even love–are brought to us by cherubs.

The next time cupid's arrow touches your heart listen for the faint flapping of tiny wings.

In the Cosmos

He bent the heavens and came down,

a dark cloud under his feet;

he mounted a cherub and flew,

and soared on the wings of the wind.

Book of Psalms 18:10-11

Whether I flie with angels, fall with dust,
Thy hands made both, and I am there:
Thy power and love, my love and trust
Make one place ev'rywhere

David Herbert Lawrence

Virgo
in
Sole
IHS
Speculum sine
Virginea generatio.

In eagerness to grow the more like Him,
Their path they follow, and succeed so far
In measure as their vison is sublime.

Dante Alighieri

Wherever the wind blows me I am taken as a welcome guest. Horace

Wherever the wind blows me I am taken as a welcome guest. Horace

With the color that paints
the morning and evening clouds
that face the sun
I saw then the whole
heaven suffused

Dante Alighieri

love is a place

& through this place of

love move

(with brightness of peace)

all places

yes is a world

& in this world of

yes live

(skilfully curled)

all worlds

e.e. cummings

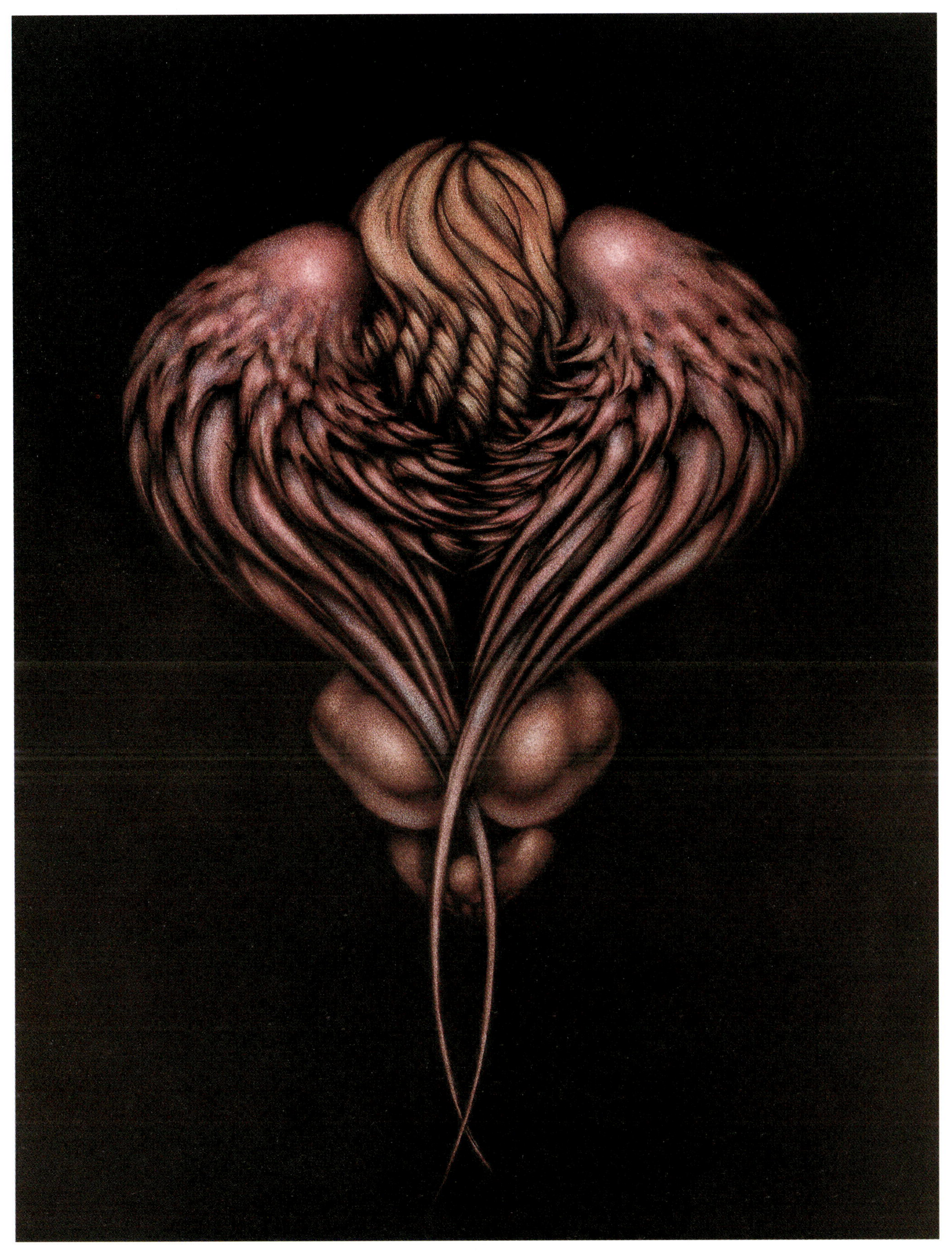

Thus passes the glory of the world

Sic transit gloria mundi

Sources

Antiques

Alfie's Antique Market
13/25 Church Street
London NW8
Tel: 071-723-0449

Architectural Salvage

Architectural & Salvage Register
46 Lots Road
London SW10
Tel: 0438-203221

Bookstores

Church Union
Faith House
7 Tufton Street
London SW1
Tel: 071-222-6952

Christian Book Centre
Kensington Temple
Kensington Park Road
London W1
Tel: 071-727-8684

Card Stores

Athena Gallery
752 High Road
London N12 9QG
Tel: 081-445-2540

Medici Gallery
7 Grafton Street
London W1
Tel: 071-837-7099

Post Impressions
146 Kings Road
London SW3 4UU
Tel: 071-589-2786

Vintage Magazine Company Ltd.
Mare Street Studios
203/213 Mare Street
London E8
Tel: 081-533-7588

Christmas Shops

The Christmas Shop
27a Mays Galleria
Tooley Street
London SE1
Tel: 071-378-1998

Christmas World Ltd.
561a Green Lanes
Harringey
London N8
Tel: 081-340-3900

Ed Wood Ltd.
Clough St. Works
Clough Street
Burnley
Tel: 0282-423069

Gisela Graham Ltd.
12 Colworth Grove
London SE17
Tel: 071-708-4956

Kent All-Year-Round Christkindlmarkt
45 Place Street
Canterbury
Kent CT1 2DZ
Tel: 0227-762525

Paper Catering Supplies Ltd.
100 Goswell Road
London EC1V
Tel: 071-253-1953

Porth 84 Ltd.
52 Great Peter Street
London SW1P
Tel: 071-222-1611

Rupert Magnus Trading Co. Plc.
Magnus House
Dukes Road
Acton
London W3 OSL
Tel: 081-993-2231

Department Stores

Harrods
Brompton Road
Knightsbridge
London SW1
Tel: 071-730-1234

Heals
196 Tottenham Court Road
London W1
Tel: 071-636-1666

Fabrics

Cecil Birtwell
71 Westbourne Park Road
London W2
Tel: 071-221-0877

Nina Campbell
9 Watton Street
London SW3
Tel: 071-225-1011

DG Distribution
26 Old Church Street
London SW3
Tel: 071-352-3111

Pierre Frey
225-253 Fulham Road
London SW3
Tel: 071-376-5599

Lelievre
16 Berners Street
London W1
Tel: 071-636-3461

Osbourne and Little
304-308 King's Road
London SW3
Tel: 071-352-1456

Timney Fowler
388 King's Road
London SW3
Tel: 071-352-2263

Watts & Co.
7 Tufton Street
London SW1
Tel: 071-222-2893

General Stores

The General Trading Co.
144 Sloane Street
London SW1
Tel: 071-730-0411

Graham and Green
4-7 & 10 Elgin Crescent
London W1
Tel: 071-727-4594

Liberty
220 Regent Street
London W1
Tel: 071-734-1234

Past Times
Witney
Oxfordshire
OX8 6BH
Tel: 0993-776490
Retail Outlets: Aberdeen, Bath, Bournemouth, Brighton, Bristol, Bromley, Cambridge, Canterbury, Cardiff, Cheltenham, Chester, Chichester, Colchester, Edinburgh, Exeter, Glasgow, Guildford, Heathrow Airport, Kingston, Knightsbridge, Leamington Spa, Liverpool, London West End, Maidstone, Norwich, Oxford, Richmond, Salisbury, Sheffield, Shrewsbury, Tunbridge Wells, Winchester, Windsor, Worcester, York

Museums

British Museum
Great Russell Street
London WC1B
Tel: 071-636-1555

National Gallery
Trafalgar Square
London WC2N
Tel: 071-839-3321

Tate Gallery
Millbank
London SW1P
Tel: 071-821-1313

Victoria and Albert Museum
Cromwell Road
London SW7
Tel: 071-938-8500

Novelty Shops

Cherubim
514 Fulham Road
London SW6
Tel: 071-736-3977

Old Curiosity Shop
13 Portsmouth Street
London WC2
Tel: 071-405-9891

Plasterworks
38 Cross Street
London N1
Tel: 071-226-5355

Paper Goods

Gallery Five Ltd.
50 Earlham Street
London WC2H
Tel: 071-836-5684

Paperchase
213 Tottenham Court Road
London W1
Tel: 071-580-8496

Pleasures of Pastimes
11 Cecil Court
London WC2
Tel: 071-836-1142

Relgious Supplies

Charles Farris
Solent House
1258 London Road
London SW16
Tel: 081-764-8777

Mission Supplies Ltd.
Alpha Place Garth Road
Morden
Surrey SM4 4LX
Tel: 081-337-0161

Vanpoulles Ltd.
1 Old Lodge Lane
Purley
Croydon CR8
Tel: 081-668-6266

Wipplell J. & Co. Ltd.
11 Tufton Street
London SW1P
Tel: 071-222-4528

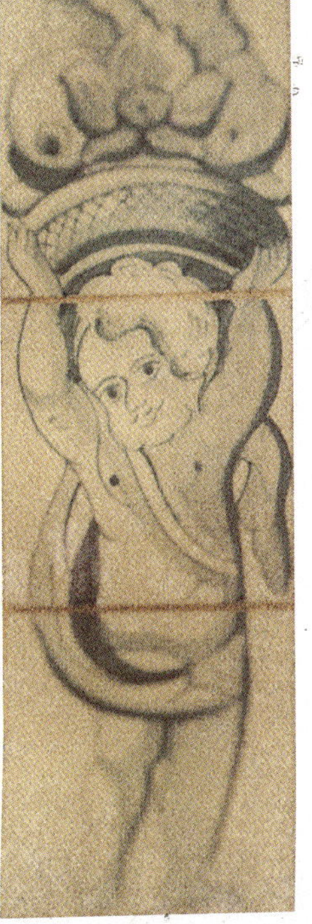

Bibliography

Select Bibliography

The author would like to record his particular debt to the following works:

Berefelt, Gunnar. *A Study on the Winged Angel.* Stockholm: Almquist & Wiksell, 1968.

Birt, Theodor. "Woher stammen die Amoretten?" In *Aus dem Leben der Antike.* Leipzig, 1919.

Davidson, Gustav. *A Dictionary of Angels Including the Fallen Angels.* New York: The Free Press, 1967.

Harrison, Jane. *Prolegomena to the Study of Greek Religion.* Cambridge: Cambridge University Press, 1903.

Lexicon Iconographicum Mythologiae Classicae, s.v. "Eros" and "Eros/Amor, Cupido." Zürich and Munich: Artemis, 1986.

Moréri, Louis. *Le Grand Dictionnaire Historique ou le Mélange curieux de l'Histoire sacrée et profane,* s.v. "Chérubins." Paris: Les Libraires Associés, 1759.

Panofsky, Erwin. *Renaissance and Renaissances in Western Art* (1960). New York: Harper & Row, 1972.

Seznec, Jean. *The Survival of the Pagan Gods; The Mythological Tradition and its Place in Renaissance Humanism and Art.* New York: Pantheon Books, 1953.

Stuveras, Roger. *Le putto dans l'art romain.* Brussels: Latomus, 1969.

Villette, Jeanne. *L'ange dans l'art d'occident du XIIème au XVIème siècle.* Paris: H. Laurens, 1940.

Weber, Siegfried. *Die Entwicklung des Putto in der Plastik der Frührenaissance.* Heidelberg, 1898.

General Bibliography

Adler, Mortimer. *Angels and Us.* New York: Macmillan, 1982.

Anderson, Joan W. *Where Angels Walk: True Stories of Heavenly Visitors.* New York: Ballentine Books, 1993.

Blazer, Howard A., Sr. *Angels, Their Origin, Nature, Mission and Destiny.* Parchment Press, 1989.

Brigidi, Stephen and Robert Bly. *Angels of Pompeii.* New York: Ballentine Books, 1992.

Burnham, Sophy. *A Book of Angels: Reflections on Angels Past and Present and True Stories of How They Touch Our Lives.* New York: Ballentine Books, 1990.

———. *Angel Letters: What You Wrote to Me.* New York: Ballantine Books, 1991.

Cameron, Betsy. *Little Angels.* New York: Villard, 1993.

Daniel, Alma, Timothy Wyllie and Andrew Ramer. *Ask Your Angels.* New York: Ballentine Books, 1992.

Freeman, Eileen Elias. *Touched by Angels.* New York: Warner Books, 1993.

Gaebelein, A. C. *What the Bible Says About Angels.* Grand Rapids, MI: Baker Book House, 1987.

Giovetti, Paola. *Angels: The Role of Celestial Guardians and Beings of Light.* New York: Weiser, 1993.

Giudici, Sr. Maria Pia. *The Angels: Spiritual and Exegetical Notes.* New York: Alba House, 1994.

Godwin, Malcolm. *Angels: An Endangered Species.* New York: Simon & Schuster, 1990.

Goldman, Karen. *The Angel Book: A Handbook for Aspiring Angels.* New York: Simon & Schuster, 1993.

———. *Angel Voices.* New York: Simon & Schuster, 1994.

Graham, Billy. *Angels: Gods Secret Agents.* New York: Random House, 1986.

Henri, Paul. *Of Men and Angels.* New York: Clarion Books, 1988.

Howard, Jane M. *Commune With the Angels: A Heavenly Handbook.* Virginia Beach, VA: ARE Press, 1992.

Humann, Harvey. *The Many Faces of Angels.* Marina del Rey, CA: DeVorss, 1987.

Long, Valentine. *Angels in Religion and Art.* Qunicy, IL: Franciscan Press, 1971.

Malz, Betty. *Angels Watching Over Me.* Grand Rapids, MI: Baker Book House, 1986.

Moolenburgh, H. C. *A Hand Book of Angels.* Essex: C. W. Daniel, 1984.

———. *Meetings With Angels: 101 Real-Life Encounters.* Essex: C.W. Daniel, 1994.

Parisien, Maria, ed. *Angels and Mortals: Their Co-Creative Power.* Wheaton, IL: Quest Books, 1990.

Ronner, John E. *Do You Have a Guardian Angel? and Other Questions Answered About Angels.* Mufreesboro, TN: Mamre Press, 1985.

———. *Know Your Angels: The Angel Almanac With Biographies of 100 Prominent Angels in Legend and Folklore.* Mufreesboro, TN: Mamre Press, 1985.

Sardello, Robert, ed. *A Gathering of Angels: Cultural Reflections on Expanding Reality.* Dallas, TX: Dallas Institute Publications, 1990.

Smith, Robert. *In the Presence of Angels.* Virginia Beach, VA: ARE Press, 1993.

Taylor, Terry L. *Messengers of Light: The Angels' Guide to Spiritual Growth.* Edited by Nancy Carleton. Tiburon, CA: H. J. Kramer, 1989.

———. *Guardians of Hope: The Angels' Guide to Personal Growth.* Edited by Nancy Carleton. Tiburon, CA: H. J. Kramer, 1992.

———.*Answers From the Angels: A Book of Angel Letters.* Tiburon, CA: H. J. Kramer, 1993.

———. *Creating With the Angels.* Tiburon, CA: H. J. Kramer, 1994.

Wilson, Peter Lamborn. *Angels: Messengers of the Gods.* London and New York: Thames and Hudson, 1994

Woody, Marilyn J. *A Child's Book of Angels: Stories From the Bible About God's Special Messengers.* Elgin, IL: Chariot Books, 1992.

Wyllie, Timothy. *Dolphins, ETs and Angels: Adventures Among Spiritual Intelligences.* Sante Fe, NM: Bear & Co. 1993.

Credits

Front Matter
Page 2 Peter Paul Rubens, *The Virgin Adored by Saints,* detail. Musee des Beaux-Arts, Grenoble, France. Page 3 John Wilkes Studio.Page 6, 7 Eric Jacobson.

Introduction
Page 12 *Cherub on a Chariot,* detail. Roman wallpainting, Casa dei Vetti, Pompeii, Italy. Scala/Art Resource, NY. *Sculpture of the River Nile,* Museo Pio Clementino, Vatican State. Page 13 *Cherubs With Garlands,* detail. Casa dei Vetti, Pompeii, Italy. Scala/Art Resource, NY. Page 14 *Crushing Grapes,* detail. Mosaic. S. Costanza, Rome, Italy. Scala/Art Resource, NY. Page 15 Francesco Traini. *The Triumph of Death,* detail of *The Garden of Love.* Camposanto, Pisa, Italy. Scala/Art Resource, NY. Raphael. *The Vision of Ezekiel.* Galleria Palatina, Palazzo Pitti, Florence, Italy. Scala/Art Resource, NY. Page 17 Raphael. *Sistine Madonna,* detail. Gemäeldegalerie, Staatliche Kunstsammlungen, Dresden, Germany. Erich Lessing/Art Resource, NY. Raphael. *Madonna di Foligno.* Pinacoteca, Vatican State. Scala/Art Resource, NY. Raphael. *The Triumph of Galatea.* Palazzo della Farnesina, Rome, Italy. Scala/Art Resource, NY. Tiziano Titian. *Assumption of the Virgin.* S. Maria Gloriosa dei Frari, Venice, Italy. Erich Lessing/Art Resource, NY. Page 18 Michelangelo. *The Prophet Isaiah.* Sistine Chapel, Vatican State. Scala/Art Resource, NY. Michelangelo. *Bacchanal of the Children.* Windsor, Windsor Castle. The Royal Collection ©1994 Her Majesty Queen Elizabeth II. Page 19 *Life,* magazine cover, March 29, 1883.

In the Heavens
Page 20-21 Gian Lorenzo Bernini. *The Cathedra of St. Peter,* detail. St. Peter's Basilica, Rome, Italy. Scala/Art Resource, NY. Page 22 George Frederick Watts (1817-1904). *Aurora.* Oldham Art Gallery, Lancaster/Bridgeman Art Library, London. Aurora. Page 23 Bartolomeo Esteban Murillo. *The Immaculate Conception,* detail. Louvre, Paris, France. Kavaler/Art Resource, NY. Ralph Waldo Emerson, from *Spirtiual Laws, Essays: First Series.* Page 24 Non aetate verum ingenio adipiscitur sapientia. Plautus, from *Trinummus.* Page 25 Rosso Fiorentino. *Madonna and Saints,* detail. Uffizi, Florence, Italy. Scala/Art Resource/NY. Page 26-27 Francois Boucher (1703-70)(studio of). *Seated Nymph With Flutes.* Wallace Collection, London/Bridgeman Art Library, London. Karl Barth, quoted in his obituary, *The New York Times,* December 11, 1986. Page 28 Carolina Lascano. Page 29 Philippe de Champaigne (1602-74). *Cherubs,* detail from *The Adoration of the Shepherds.* Wallace Collection, London. Bridgeman Art Library, London. Page 30-31 Nicolas Rene Jollain (1732-1804). *Sleeping Child (Le Sommeil),* detail. Wallace Collection, London/Bridgeman Art Library, London. Propertius, from *Elegies.*

Visits and Messengers
Page 32-33 Janet Atkinson. *Angel With Telephone.* Page 34 Eric Jacobson. Page 36-37 Lesley Ehlers. Page 38-39 Alexandre Cabanel(1823-89), *Birth of Venus 1863,* Musee d'Orsay, Paris/Giraudon/Bridgeman Art Library, London. Baron Friedrich von Hardenberg, from *Blutenstaub (Pollen).* Page 40 *The Emperor Shah Jahan Standing Upon a Globe.* India, mid.17th century, Mughal, school of Shah Jahan. By Hashim. Color and gold on paper: 25.7 x 15.8 cm, Courtesy of the Freer Gallery of Art, Smithsonian Institution, Washington, D.C.(39.49a). Photo by James T. Hayden. Page 41 *Glorification of Akbar, with Lion and Heifer.* From an album of 37 leaves, assembled for Emperor Shah Jahan. By Govardhan. Colors and gilt on paper. © The Metropolitan Museum of Art, Purchase, Rogers Fund and The Kevorkian Foundation Gift, 1955. (55.121.10.22). Page 42 Barry Rosenthal. Sculpture courtesy Tim McKoy Gallery, NY. Page 43 William Blake, from *Poems From Blake's Notebook, Love to Faults.* Page 44-45 *Life* magazine, January 18, 1906, Vol XLVII, No. 1212. John Donne, from *The Sun Rising.* Page 46 Peter de Sève. Page 47 Mark Hill. Weathervane courtesy of Recherchè of Gramercy Park, NY. Robert Burton, from *The Anatomy of Melancholy.* Page 48 *Shah Shuja Enthroned With Gaj Singh of Marwar,* detail. India, c. 1633-1638. The Nasli and Alice Heeramaneck Collection, Museum Associates Purchase, Los Angeles County Museum of Art (M.80.6.6). Henry Vaughan, from *(They are all gone into the world of light!).* Page 49 Shah Shuja enthroned with Gaj Singh of Marwar. India, C. 1633-1638. Opaque watercolors on paper: 25.1 x 17.5 cm. The Nasli and Alice Heeramaneck Collection, Museum Associates Purchase, Los Angeles County Museum of Art (M.80.6.6).

Music and Play
Page 50-51 Donatello. *Cantoria,* detail. Museo dell'Opera del Duomo, Florence, Italy. Scala/Art Resource, NY. Page 52 Mark Hill. Sculpture courtesy of Wolfman, Gold & Good Company, NY. Page 53 Mark Hill. Ornament courtesy of At Home on Christopher, NY. Samuel Taylor Coleridge, from *Hymn Before Sun-Rise in the Vale of Chamouni.* Page 54-55 Unknown artist. *The Holy Family with Angels.* Oil on Canvas, 39 x 89 1/2-in., International Institute of Iberian Colonial Art, University of New Mexico, L. 87.3.30. Photo by Damian Andru. Urania Bailey, from *I Want to be an Angel.* Page 56 Agostino di Duccio. *Angel Musicians.* Tempio Malatestiano, Rimini, Italy. Scala/Art Resource, NY. Page 58-59 Barry Rosenthal. Edgar Allan Poe, from *Israfel.* Page 60-61 Rosso Fiorentino. *Musical Angel.* Uffizi, Florence, Italy. Scala/Art Resource, NY. William Shakespeare, *Love's Labour's Lost.* Page 62-63 Peter Michelena. Richard Crashaw, from *Saint Mary Magdalene.*

Lovers and Fertility
Page 64, 65 Detail and card, *Angel of the Tarot de Marseille.* Page 64, 65 Detail and card, Angel of the Tarot de Marseille, © B.P. Grimaud 1981. Reproduced with the kind authorization of France Cartes BP 49—54130 Saint Max, France. Page 66 *Life* magazine, February 10, 1910. Page 67 Sir Walter Ralegh, from *As You Caome From the Holy Land.* Page 70 George Santayana, *The Life of Reason, vol II, Reason in Society.* Page 71 Cranach, Lucas the Elder. *Venus.* Galleria Borghese, Rome Italy. Scala/Art Resource, NY. Page 72-73 Peter Paul Rubens. *The Garden of Love.* Prado, Madrid, Spain. Giraudon/Art Resource, NY. Fulke Greville, Lord Brooke, from *Caelica and Philocell.* Page 76 William Shakespeare, from *A Midsummer-Night's Dream.* Page 77 Sandro Botticelli(1444/5-1510). *Primavera: Detail of Cupid.* Galleria degli Uffizi, Florence/Bridgeman Art Library, London, Outside gatefold Raphael. *The Triumph of Galatea,* detail. Palazzo della Farnesina, Rome, Italy. Scala, Art Resource, NY. Fulke Greville, Lord Brooke, from *Cynthia.* Inside gatefold Charles Antoine Coypel(1694-1752). *Armide Wishing to Hit Renaud.,* Musee des Beaux-Arts, Nantes/Giraudon/Bridgeman Art Library, London. Page 84 Peter Paul Rubens. *Madonna and Child With Angels,* detail. Louvre, Paris, France. Scala/Art Resource, New York. Page 85 Francois Boucher (1703-70) (follower of), *Amorini* (red chalk), Wallace Collection, London/Bridgeman Art Library, London. Edmund Waller, from *Upon the Death of My Lady Rich.* Page 87 Jean-Baptiste Huet (1745-1811). *Cupid Commemorating a Marriage by Incising on a Tablet the Interlaced Initials FT and RC, 1797.* Christie's, London/Bridgeman Art Library, London. Page 89 Jacques Charlier(c. 1705-90). *The Birth of Venus* (after Boucher). Wallace Collection, London/Bridgeman Art Library, London. George Birdseye, from *Godey's Lady's Book.*

Mischief and Play
Page 90-91 Giulio Romano. Rustic Banquet, detail. Palazzo del Te', Mantua, Italy. Scala/Art Resource, NY. Page 92 *Beware!,* from *Life* magazine February 6, 1902. Page 93 Peter Paul Rubens. *The Holy Family Under an Apple Tree,* detail. Kunsthistorisches Museum, Vienna. Art Resource, NY. Page 94 William-Adolphe Bouguereau (1825-1905). *The Birth of Venus,* detail. Musee d'Orsay, Paris/Bridgeman Art Library, London. Page 95 Andrea Verrocchio. *Putto With Dolphin, in Front Courtyard.* Palazzo Vecchio, Florence, Italy. Scala/Art Resource, NY. Richard Wilbur, from *Advice to a Prophet.* Page 96 Samuel Butler, from *God is Love.* Page 97 Andy Warhol. Jacket designed for Ronald Firbank's *Three More Novels,* courtsey of New Directions Publishing Corporation.Page 98-99 Tiziano Titian (called Vecellio) (c.1485-1576). *The Worship of Venus, 1519,* detail. Prado, Madrid/Bridgeman Art Library, London. Dylan Thomas, from *Fern Hill.* Page 100 Paul Verlaine. *Cupid Fallen.* From *Paul Verlaine: Selected Poems,* trans./ed. by C. F. MacIntyre, © 1948 The Regents of the University of California. Page 103 Angelica Kauffman (1741-1807). *An Allegory of Sculpture.* Cheltenham Art Gallery & Museums, Glos./Bridgeman Art Library, London. Page 104-105 Fred Winkowski.

In the Cosmos
Page 106-107 Raphael. (school of). *Cherub Riding a Chariot Pulled by Snails.* Stufetta del Card. Bibbiena, Vatican Palace, Vatican State. Scala/Art Resource, NY. Page 108 Inclinavit caelos et descendit, et caligo sub pedibus eius, et ascendit super cherubim et volavit; volavit super pennas ventorum. Book of Psalms 18: 10-11. Page 109 Raphael. *The Vision of Ezekiel.* Galleria Palatina, Palazzo Pitti, Florence, Italy. Scala, Art Resource, NY. Page 110, 111 Mark Hill. Budda courtesy of Recherche of Gramercy Park, NY. David Herbert Lawrence, from *Song of a Man Who Has Come Through.* Page 112 Antonio Vilca. *Misterio de la Encarnación.* Museo Histórico Regional, Cuzco, Peru. Page 113 Dante Alighieri, from *The Divine Comedy, Paradise.* Page 114-115 *Putti* fabric courtesy of Schumacher, NY. Quo me cumque rapit tempestas deferor hospes. Horace, from *Epistles.* Page 116-117 Eric Jacobson. Dante Alighieri, from *The Divine Comedy, Paradise.* Page 118 e.e. cummings. *love is a place.* From *Complete Poems, 1904-62,* ed. by George J. Firmage, © 1935, 1963, 1991 by the Trustees for the e.e. cummings Trust, used by permission of Liveright Publishing Corporation. Page 119 Greg Michaelson. Page 120 Raphael. *Ceiling of the Stanza della Segnatura, detail: Astronomy.* Vatican Palace, Vatican State. Scala/Art Resource, NY. Page 121 Raphael. *Ceiling of the the Stanza della Segnatura, detail: Justice.* Vatican Palace, Vatican State. Scala/Art Resource, NY. Page 125 Mark Hill. Portugeuse cherub panel courtesy of Country Tiles, NY.

Cover: Philippe de Champaigne (1602-74). *Cherubs,* detail from *The Adoration of the Shepherds.* Wallace Collection, London/The Bridgeman Art Library, London. Raphael. *The Triumph of Galatea,* detail. Palazzo della Farnesina, Rome, Italy. Scala/Art Resource, NY. Rosso Fiorentino. *Madonna and Saints,* detail. Uffizi, Florence, Italy. Scala/Art Resource, NY.

We have strived to obtain the necessary permission for reproduction of the illustrations contained within these pages and to provide the proper copyright credits. We would appreciate notification on any error or omission, which we will amend in all subsequent printings.

Index